I0037240

Regulatory Compliance Fundamentals

M.L. HUMPHREY

All statements in this book are those of the author and the author only. They should not be construed to reflect the views or opinions of any other entity, including any former employer.

Copyright © 2020 M.L. Humphrey
All Rights Reserved.
ISBN: 978-1-950902-22-4

SELECT TITLES BY M.L. HUMPHREY

How to Gather and Use Data For Business Analysis

Regulatory Compliance Fundamentals

AML Compliance Fundamentals

* * *

Budgeting for Beginners

Excel for Budgeting

* * *

Excel for Beginners

Word for Beginners

PowerPoint for Beginners

Access for Beginners

CONTENTS

CONTENTS (CONT.)

INTRODUCTION

We live in a regulated world. Some industries are far more regulated than others.

And for good reason, I think. I personally have no desire to get botulism from a can of food or have my car lose steering while I'm driving down the highway. Nor do I want someone to be able to take my money when I deposit it at the bank. And I'd certainly like my grandma's prescription medications to be consistent and free of toxins.

Ideally, companies would do these things on their own because it's good business to not steal from, poison, or otherwise endanger your customers. But harsh experience has shown that's not how the world works. So we have regulations that all businesses must comply with, like tax regulations and employment laws, and then there are the industry-specific requirements where generally the more risk to the eventual customer, the more regulation.

And while it can initially seem straight-forward to comply with these regulations, my almost twenty years of experience with regulation in the financial services industry has shown me that it is not. For many businesses, especially smaller businesses operating in a highly-regulated environment, the scope and pace of regulation can be overwhelming. For larger businesses it's usually more an issue of how best to build a compliance program that is effective yet still cost-conscious.

So what I've tried to do in this book is lay out a framework for how to approach regulatory compliance and the different ways in which that compliance can be achieved.

I'm an opinionated person, so I'll also touch on a few issues that aren't specifically regulatory compliance issues. For example, right up front we'll discuss compliance as a business decision and what that means to everyone within the organization. I'll also touch on some concepts that originated in auditing and have found their way into compliance, such as tone at the top. And how industry best practices and regulatory guidance can skew the actual written requirements that apply to your company.

All of this is part and parcel of regulatory compliance in my opinion. Although there is also the basic framework of how to approach compliance that we'll cover as well.

At this point you're probably wondering who I am and why you should listen to me. What gives me the experience to write this book?

My background is in financial services regulation.

Regulatory Compliance Fundamentals

I started my career at what was then NASD, now FINRA, which is a government-authorized entity in the United States that is responsible for the primary oversight of broker-dealers based in or doing business in the United States. (The Securities and Exchange Commission (SEC) then provides oversight of them, but the majority of on-site examinations of broker-dealers conducted in the U.S. are conducted by FINRA examiners.)

I was initially a field examiner, conducting on-site exams of broker-dealers for compliance with FINRA as well as SEC requirements. I then worked in the department at FINRA that was responsible for writing the examination procedures for all of those field examiners. During that time I wrote or rewrote FINRA's examination procedures for anti-money laundering (AML) regulation, mutual fund compliance, and a number of other regulatory requirements, although I'm certain they've changed since then. I was also one of their designated national experts on anti-money laundering regulation.

When I left FINRA I went to work for a boutique consulting firm where I worked with a large range of financial services entities from broker-dealers to banks to money services businesses to investment advisors to credit rating agencies and more. My focus was on anti-money laundering compliance, credit rating agency regulations, and corporate governance and risk compliance.

My clients at the consulting firm were some of the largest financial institutions in the world, and we often evaluated their compliance programs on an entity-wide basis so I also ended up dealing with regulatory requirements from all over the world.

After I left full-time salaried employment I continued to work with a large range of clients and on a wide variety of projects, including a number that dealt with data. For example, one project involved the standardization of data across multiple internal platforms. Another involved providing a subject matter review of a data set to determine what data it actually contained and what the limitations of that data set were. (I'll touch on data issues a bit in this book, but I explored them more thoroughly in *How to Gather and Use Data for Business Analysis* formerly published as *Data Principles for Beginners*.)

So that's me.

All told I spent close to twenty years on regulatory compliance in the financial services industry with experience on both the compliance and the regulatory side, which I think is essential when trying to discuss this topic in the way we're going to for the rest of this book.

I guess I should add here that I also triple majored at Stanford (in Anthropology, Psychology, and Economics) and have an MBA from the Wharton School at the University of Pennsylvania.

Although I honestly will tell you that formal education is meaningless when it comes to being knowledgeable about regulatory compliance. It's very much a boots on the ground area of expertise. I just mention it so that we can get the trust factor out of the way because my default style of communication is more casual than my experience or education would imply.

This is a fairly short book, because the basic framework of regulatory compliance is pretty simple and straight-forward. I like to say it's not rocket science.

Having said that, though, the trade-offs and real-life judgement calls that have to be made when you're dealing with regulatory compliance are anything but simple. That's where experience and expertise truly come into play. So what I'm giving you here is the foundation you need to build from. How you put that into practice day-to-day will depend very much on your industry and the specific company you work for.

You may be wondering at this point if this book is for you. And I would say that if you have an interest in regulatory compliance, no matter your level of expertise or industry, then, yes, it is. Many of the examples I'm going to use are based on my experience in the financial services industry and more specifically AML compliance, but I've tried to make this book accessible to anyone tasked with building, managing, participating in, or regulating a regulatory compliance program.

Alright then.

Now that you have a general idea of what we're going to cover and who I am, let's dive right in starting with one of the most controversial aspects of regulatory compliance: the fact that at the end of the day compliance is a business decision.

COMPLIANCE AS A BUSINESS DECISION

As someone who started my career on the regulatory side of the business I would love to think that all companies strive to comply with all of their regulatory requirements with 100% effort and dedication. But that is not the case.

Nor is it possible.

Let's take a very simple example from broker-dealer regulation, discretionary accounts.

FINRA has a rule, FINRA Rule 3260, related to discretionary accounts. These are accounts where the customer has granted their broker the right to enter into transactions on their behalf without specific permission from the customer.

If a discretionary account exists, additional supervision and documentation are required.

The rule has an exception for trades where the stock and quantity of shares have been approved by the customer but the price and timing are left up to the broker.

So if Gary Broker talks to his customer at nine in the morning and says, "I think we should buy 100 shares of Disney today" and the customer says, "Okay", Gary could wait a little bit to put in that purchase order trying to get the best price as long as the customer knows he is going to do so and that would not be considered exercising discretion.

But he can't wait until the next day to put in the order. And he certainly can't just put through a trade in a customer's account without calling them.

Seems straight-forward enough, right? Unless the account is discretionary, the customer needs to approve that transaction on that day.

But how would you ensure compliance with this requirement *with 100% certainty*?

You could call every customer and confirm that they'd authorized the order.

You could require a customer signature or email on all orders unless a discretionary agreement was in place.

You could have real-time monitoring of all customer communications to make sure that all transactions were authorized.

Or you could have the broker transfer the customer to a different staff member to confirm approval.

I'm sure there are a few other options that would serve the same purpose as well. But that's a lot of effort to monitor for something that is not very common.

Many of the small broker-dealers (or firms) I examined twenty years ago "complied" with this rule by stating in their policies and procedures that they didn't allow discretionary accounts. But they failed to even define what that was. (Which really was not sufficient.)

The only firms that actually monitored their transactions to the extent mentioned above were ones that were required to do so as a result of a settlement with their regulator. Or ones who fell under a very specific separate regulatory requirement (the "Taping Rule") that was meant to capture firms where "bad brokers" had moved.

The rest of the broker-dealers fell somewhere in between those two extremes. And where they fell on that spectrum was a business decision.

Every broker-dealer evaluated its business, the types of customers it serviced, and the types of brokers it employed, and then made a decision about how to comply with this requirement while still remaining competitive within the industry.

This happens with every single rule in every single regulated industry.

Whether anyone wants to admit it or not, businesses analyze all regulatory compliance decisions from a risk and cost perspective. How much will it cost us to do this? How much trouble will we get into if we don't do it?

I would be willing to bet money that the full analysis rarely gets put in writing, however, because stupid people don't stay in business long. And no one wants to have a written document at their company that outlines why they determined they didn't need to ensure full compliance with a regulation that was meant to prevent theft or endangering someone's life.

So no one puts this full analysis in writing. But these are the types of questions they ask:

How relevant is this requirement to our business? Does it apply to 100% of our business? Does it only apply to 1% of our business?

How costly is it to comply with this requirement? Are there alternatives that are less costly? What do we risk with the lower-cost alternatives?

How important is this requirement to our shareholders? Our regulator? Our board? Our customers? Our employees? And the public?

What are the consequences if we don't comply? Will people die? Will people lose their money? Will we be sued by our customers? Will our regulator take action against us?

There are also a few questions I wish weren't part of the analysis that rarely get voiced, but are absolutely present for some individuals:

How long will it take for someone to figure out that we didn't comply? Can someone figure it out? If so, can they tie it back to me individually? Will I pay a personal cost for that failure to comply?

How much more money can we make if we don't comply? Will we "win" over our competition if we cut this corner?

There are also questions I wish were more a part of the analysis than I think they are:

What is the reputational risk to our company of not complying with this requirement?

What other non-financial consequences could there be to our not complying?

Are there non-regulatory requirements that we

should be taking into account when we make this decision?

Are we willing to have our business associated with this type of issue? Could being associated with this type of issue end our company?

(And if you don't think that's possible, I suggest you look up what happened with Riggs Bank and its AML issues or Arthur Andersen after the Enron scandal. Compliance issues can end your company as you know it.)

(I will also add here that certain industries and certain portions of industries are much more sensitive to reputational risk than others. I had three friends of mine who are still very active in financial services regulation read through an earlier version of this book for me. One objected to my characterization above about reputational risk not being considered enough. This individual has worked largely with insurance-focused financial institutions and said reputational risk is always a key consideration. And I would agree that that's probably true for most entities in that part of the financial services industry. But there are most definitely other industries and other parts of the financial services industry where reputation was not considered enough based on the choices that those entities subsequently made.)

So those are the types of questions that arise when making a decision about how to fund or create a regulatory compliance program. There is no way to make decisions about your regulatory compliance program without factoring in competitiveness and cost.

The "business" side of the company will always focus on those factors.

And compliance is always going to hear statements like: How much is this going to inconvenience my people? How much will it get in the way of my making the sales I need to make? If I have to do X and the competition doesn't, I'll lose.

This puts the compliance staff in a very difficult position. In a highly-regulated industry, compliance staff will not only feel the pressure from the business to "lighten up and get out of the way" but they will also feel the pressure from their regulator to fully comply with each and every regulation.

It takes a certain interpersonal skill and obstinacy to successfully navigate that balance. Cave to the business and the company ends up paying for that with regulatory fines and reputational hits. Take too hard a line with the business, find yourself cut out of decisions where you need to be involved, assuming you aren't quietly pushed out the door.

There is always going to be that tension between meeting regulatory requirements and being competitive and profitable. Compliance needs to be the voice in the room reminding everyone that there are consequences for non-compliance even if those consequences aren't going to be seen for years. But they also need to be creative in finding the best way to comply with the requirements without handicapping the business.

What about the regulators? How should they

approach things knowing this about the entities they regulate?

Well...

That's more tricky. At the higher levels of every regulator I've ever dealt with, there was a political consideration that had to be made. Because if you insist on 100% perfect compliance with every single regulation every single day, you create an impossible expectation. Not to mention the resources required to enforce that.

Think about when people drive their cars and they speed. Can you imagine what it would take to ensure 100% compliance with speed limits throughout the country? On all roads at all times? Can you imagine how people would feel towards law enforcement if that were to actually happen?

So there's a balance there, too. But my opinion is that on the regulatory side the regulator's role is to keep the pressure on and hold the line. The requirements are the requirements and they all exist for a reason.

But some are more serious than others. And some violations are clearly not intentional. So that should be taken into account when deciding what level of action to pursue for a violation.

When I was a field examiner there were some items I'd just point out verbally to a firm, some that we'd cite in the exit interview or the written letter that closed out the exam, and some where we'd make the firm pay a fine.

If someone had made a good faith effort to comply, it was usually just the letter. But if customers were harmed? Or the issue was high impact (like money laundering was at the time)? Or the firm kept ignoring the requirement? Well, that needed to be treated more seriously.

So, in summary:

Understand that every single business's compliance program will be driven by business considerations, and that there is no way to ensure 100% compliance with all regulations at all times. But that each person has their role to play to keep the appropriate amount of tension in the system to make sure that most regulations are followed most of the time and that the really important ones (that impact customer well-being) are followed almost all the time.

Now that we understand that, let's talk regulatory requirements.

DETERMINING YOUR REGULATORY REQUIREMENTS

It seems straight-forward enough to figure out what your regulatory requirements are, right? You just look at the regulations that apply to your industry, identify the ones that apply to your business, and then comply with those.

Well, yes and no.

That is absolutely a good start. Broker-dealers that are registered with FINRA know they need to comply with FINRA's rules. But they also need to comply with certain SEC regulations. And if they do municipal securities, rules issued by the Municipal Securities Rulemaking Board (MSRB). And pretty much every U.S.-based business needs to comply with Office of Foreign Assets Control (OFAC) regulations as well as treasury regulations related to the handling of cash transactions.

So right there we have more than four potential sets of rules or regulations that apply to a broker-dealer. If they do insurance products, like variable annuities, then that brings in a whole slew of other regulations since the insurance industry is regulated at the state level.

And if they also provide investment advisory services, depending on the size of that business, they either have another set of SEC regulations to comply with or another set of state-level regulations that come into play.

Plus, if they conduct international business now they're looking at complying with the rules or regulations that apply in each and every country where they conduct operations. Sometimes that will only be countries where they have an office, but often that can be countries where customers are located or countries where a certain volume of business is conducted. (Just ask any online retailer about customer data protection.)

As you can see, the list gets very long very fast.

And you'll note that what I didn't cover above was anything related to employment law or taxes. Because in a traditional compliance department, those types of rules and regulations are not covered under the compliance program.

At a senior management level they should be considered as part of operational risk assessments. (If we get sued because the CEO slept with his secretary, what will that do to our share price?) But in general, HR and tax and those sorts of regulations are not incorporated into a regulatory compliance program.

So you put together your list of rules and regulations. (If this is a new industry for you this is a good time to hire a law firm or a consulting firm who already knows what rules and regulations apply so they can short-cut this process for you.)

And then the fun begins.

Because if you have a business that is conducted in multiple jurisdictions with overlapping rules and regulations you now have a decision to make. Do you comply with the highest standard everywhere? Or do you allow regional variation so that each business unit in each jurisdiction complies only with the local requirements?

Which direction you choose to go will impact corporate structure as well as all of your policies, procedures, and monitoring systems.

I mentioned earlier that I'd worked on credit rating agency regulation. That is a perfect example of this type of issue.

I spent an entire year mapping the requirements for credit rating agencies across the various countries where my client had operations, trying to figure out, for example, for each Japanese credit rating agency regulation which EU regulation was its equivalent and then which US regulation was equivalent to those two.

Mapping those requirements was step one, but then we had to evaluate how those requirements were the same and how they differed. Were they requiring the same thing, but just using different words? Or did one require far more monitoring and reporting than the others?

Let me assure you, that was not easy. Because the terminology between each jurisdiction differed and how they chose to structure their regulations also differed. You could not rely on the same requirements being placed in the same location in each set of regulations.

For each identified requirement we assisted our client in determining whether it would be better to comply with the higher standard across all countries or to only comply regionally. For those requirements that were so onerous it was best to just comply regionally, then the client had to determine if they had the appropriate legal and supervisory structure in place to do that.

Fortunately, most industries are not subject to completely new regulation and over time these things shake themselves out and become more similar across jurisdictions. Although not always. And often one jurisdiction will start to increase regulations before another. For an example, just look at the current data protection requirements in the EU versus the U.S.

If you're in a newly-regulated industry or one where a new area of regulation is quickly evolving, this can be a challenging time. There are no simple decisions. And what makes sense in January can no longer make sense by April as requirements continue to evolve.

Even in more established industries attitudes and regulatory focus can change over time. So rules and regulations need to be monitored by someone knowledgeable enough to know when a change will impact the business.

(I should note here that the monitoring role may fall outside of the compliance department, especially in larger organizations. Often Legal is responsible for this role.)

Also, because the process of writing new rules or regulations is often a long and complex one, businesses need to monitor not just the wording of the rules and regulations that apply to them, but they also need to monitor changing regulatory expectations. This is why being a member of industry groups and keeping in contact with your peers at other organizations is crucial to long-term success. You need to know how regulatory expectations are changing in your industry.

This is especially true in an industry that is governed by a principles-based regulatory system.

Let me take a moment to define that. A principles-based regulatory system tends to have fewer but higher-level regulations. So there might be a requirement to "deal with customers fairly" but no specific rule or regulation that says what that means.

Well then, what does that mean? Does it mean that you tell your customer everything you know about a transaction? Does it mean that you can't do something for yourself unless you also do it for them? Does it mean that you can only charge so much for your services? Does it mean that you must disclose every payment you receive in connection with the services you offer them?

All good questions.

And what generally happens with a principles-based regulatory system is that over time cases are brought or guidance is issued that define what the principles actually mean. So over time a principles-based regulatory system starts to look more and more like a rules-based regulatory system. And sometimes it will even evolve into one as that guidance becomes codified into rules.

So a business may think it has an understanding of the rules and regulations that apply to it, but those requirements may evolve over time. Something that everyone in the industry does may become unacceptable in the eyes of the public or of the regulator and the business will need to adjust when that happens.

(And I will tell you now that "everyone else was doing it" is seldom a sufficient defense if a regulator finds a rule they can hang a violation on, especially if what was being done was questionable enough to alarm a reasonable person.)

Even in industries that have extensive rules, like the financial services industry where I come from, regulatory guidance and regulatory actions are a crucial element of defining what businesses are actually expected to do.

For example, FINRA publishes Regulatory Notices, some of which provide additional interpretation of its rules, as well as issuing Interpretive Letters that answer specific questions about how a rule applies to a specific set of facts.

In addition, members of FINRA's leadership give speeches at industry conferences highlighting examination priorities, and FINRA also publishes an annual list of exam priorities and a monthly list of disciplinary actions it has taken.

All of this, even though it may not be documented in a rule, should be used in evaluating the sufficiency of a regulatory compliance program. Those businesses that don't pay attention to this sort of guidance risk regulatory action.

On top of all of that is one more issue that businesses need to be aware of, and that's industry best practices. If you are the only one of your peers who is not doing something, then you are in jeopardy of being seen as non-compliant even if there is no specific rule or regulation that requires that particular action.

Let me give an example from the world of anti-money laundering requirements.

FINRA member firms range in size from one-man firms with a handful of clients up to firms that employ tens of thousands of individuals and are responsible for trillions of dollars in assets. It is not reasonable to expect that a one-man firm have an AML program that is as advanced or robust as the largest firms in the industry.

The one-man firm can probably get away with manually reviewing customer activity and is very unlikely to have customers in high-risk jurisdictions so isn't going to be expected to have a robust automated monitoring system that flags that type of customer.

And that one-man firm can also probably get away with only monitoring activity on a monthly basis. (Although if some significant transaction were to occur that was suspicious, the regulator would expect that to be noticed immediately since it's such a small firm.)

Compare that to the largest firms in the industry. They absolutely need a sophisticated monitoring system that incorporates jurisdictional risk, likely generating activity alerts daily, monthly, and quarterly that are reviewed by subject matter experts in a dedicated department.

Somewhere between those two extremes firms should move from a manual monitoring process to an automated one. But where does that line exist? When is a firm suddenly big enough or dealing with high enough risk clients that they need to use sophisticated, automated monitoring? That's not set out in the rules or regulations that apply to AML.

It is a facts and circumstances determination that is made based upon an analysis of what other firms are doing, what is considered reasonable given the size of the firm and their business mix, and the seriousness of anything that was missed by not having an adequate system in place.

So a firm whose peers have all established a system of sophisticated monitoring that fails to do so itself puts itself at risk of a regulatory action for not being in line with current industry best practice. *Even if the rules aren't that specific about what they should do.*

Which means not only should a compliance program look at the written rules and regulations, it should also look at the interpretation and guidance on those rules, and it should look at what industry practice is with respect to all of those rules and regulations.

Not only that, it should be a program that is changing and dynamic and that is built to incorporate new regulations, new expectations, and new advancements in industry best practice, collectively the regulatory requirements for the business.

Ideally, a regulatory compliance program should be just on the upper edge of compliance compared to a business's peers. You don't want to be behind the curve, but you don't want to spend so much that you are too far ahead of the curve either because that is likely to put you at a competitive disadvantage.

(Keep in mind, though, that technology systems cannot be implemented in a day. Most take months if not years to fully implement. So you may have to be ahead of the curve initially to be in line with your peers or keep from falling behind later.)

I should also note here one more issue that I ran into a few years ago.

This is for the fast-moving, tech-savvy among you. And that is that it is possible to get too far ahead of your regulatory requirements and end up in violation because you were trying to be too innovative.

At an alumni event I attended someone was complaining to me about a problem they'd run into trying to expand banking in Africa. Rather than rely on physical customer identification they wanted to use biometrics to identify their customers. But they were stopped by their regulator because for AML customer identification purposes biometrics were not an acceptable form of identification.

This company was ahead of the curve in how they wanted to identify their customers, which was just as bad from the regulatory perspective as not having a program in place at all.

Sure, it might have made sense given the nature of that client base to use biometrics since people weren't going to have driver's licenses or passports to present, but…The rules are the rules. And they were not made to accommodate biometric identification.

The only way to deal with a situation like that is to ask for a rule interpretation so that you have official approval to do what you want.

You could try to get the rule amended, but that is not always an easy thing to do and in that particular case would have required extensive coordination across a number of regulators and perhaps jurisdictions.

Or you can just follow the rule as it currently exists even if it isn't the best solution. Rules and regulations rarely are.

So, in summary. Know all the written rules and regulations that apply to your business. Know the interpretations and case law around those rules and regulations. And know where the industry is in terms of attitudes and best practices. Those taken together make up your regulatory requirements.

And then make sure to monitor all of the above for changes and adjust your compliance program accordingly. A compliance program is not and should never be a static program. It must adjust to changing circumstances.

POLICIES, PROCEDURES, GUIDELINES, AND OPERATIONS MANUALS

As far as I know these terms are not precisely defined. When we were building the compliance program for our credit rating agency client we established what each one was for that purpose, but things can be a little more fluid across companies.

When I was an examiner for FINRA we usually asked to see the policies and procedures at a firm. We might occasionally want to see an operations manual, but not as often.

So what were we looking for?

We wanted to see a written document that was generally available to all registered personnel that set forth the regulatory requirements that applied to that business and how they complied with them on a moderately high level, including assignment of supervisory duties to specific individuals.

We did not expect in that document to see how to make the specific entries in a system to complete a task. That's what an operations manual is for. What we wanted was to see that someone had been assigned to do that task.

Let's go back to that example I used before related to discretionary accounts. As I mentioned, a lot of the firms I examined had policies and procedures that said, "Discretionary accounts are not allowed at XYZ firm."

Okay.

Well, what is a discretionary account? Do you expect your employees to know that when you haven't given them a rule reference nor have you defined it?

When I was an examiner one of the cases I brought against a broker was because that broker's firm had a policy that said these types of accounts were not allowed, but that failed to define what a discretionary account was. So this broker thought that talking to a client and providing them a list of ten different stocks that he *might* buy for them that month was allowed. It wasn't.

Because the customer didn't authorize the purchase of *one* of the specific stocks on that list, that was not considered appropriate authorization. Also, because the conversation did not happen on the day of the transaction it did not fall under the time and price discretion exception.

The firm didn't provide enough information in their policies and procedures for that representative to comply. Nor did the firm make any additional effort to monitor for compliance with the requirement, which ultimately resulted in a fine against both the representative and the firm.

A better set of policies and procedures would have started with the policy that the firm does not allow discretionary accounts. It would have also included a citation of the rule or regulatory guidance that applied. And it would have also provided a brief description of what a discretionary account was or was not.

In an ideal world, even though a firm had said they didn't allow that type of account, you'd also see what steps they'd follow if such an account were found to exist. But that last one would probably be allowed to slide if it wasn't there.

Also, the firm would have established some way to document or verify that its representatives were aware of this requirement. And if it was instead a requirement that did apply to the business they would have established steps to supervise for compliance.

So, to recap: What is the requirement? How do we choose to comply with it? Who is responsible for that compliance? What basic information do employees need to know to understand the requirement? What high-level steps are we taking to supervise for compliance, if necessary?

What does not need to be listed are the step-by-step instructions for how to perform that compliance monitoring. Not every employee needs to know how the secret sauce is made. They need to know the requirements that apply to them and to be given enough information to act accordingly.

How a business monitors for compliance can vary and we'll discuss that more in the section titled *Your Compliance Tools*.

Also, remember that your industry may be evolving. What was fine in policies and procedures five years ago may not be today. Or what I outlined above may not be sufficient for your industry. They may want everything in the policies and procedures document.

You should have enough information somewhere to let you complete all of your monitoring duties. If you are trying to document compliance with your regulatory requirements, that needs to in fact be documented. You need to be able to show someone what you did and when and why. And you need to support your policies and procedures with operations or department-level manuals that make sure that things are done the way they need to be.

Your policies and procedures should cover your regulatory requirements in sufficient detail that someone can understand them from a high-level perspective and know the basic steps you are taking to comply with each one. But the step-by-step day-to-day operational information can be in a department-level document, just do make sure that it's actually documented.

It may seem obvious, but your policies and procedures should in fact be written.

A NOTE ON CORPORATE
STRUCTURE AND TONE AT THE TOP

Here is a simple fact: People do what they're rewarded for. So if the president of the company doesn't care about compliance, your employees won't either. And if their immediate boss says, "Who cares about XYZ requirement, I want to see you hit your numbers" that's what that employee is going to do.

The management and board of the company set the tone for compliance. If all management communication is about revenue generation and profit, that's where the focus of all of the employees will be. So you can have a beautifully written compliance manual that says everything it should say, but if employees aren't expected to comply with what it says, that is so much worthless paper.

Which leads to the question, how do you convey to employees that regulatory compliance is important?

One way to do so, of course, would be to have the head of the company not just talk about profitability for the quarter, but safety or the low number of customer complaints received or how proud they are of the industry award for being considered trustworthy. That's one way.

(Although, be careful that talking about customer complaints doesn't lead to someone just finding a way to keep those from coming to management's attention, which I have seen happen. Those weren't *complaints,* they were just negative customer correspondence...)

Another way to do so is to make sure that the board or senior management is receiving reports on compliance matters and paying attention to them. This falls under the general heading of board reporting, although if you don't have a board it can just be reporting to senior management.

Metrics that are reported will probably vary by industry, but in financial services I liked to see reports on the number of complaints received each quarter, the type of complaints being received (operational vs. sales practice and what type of sales practice), the types of products that were subject to a complaint, etc. Also, perhaps new product approvals and discussion. Pending regulatory matters. Transaction monitoring statistics including how many alerts were generated, how many were reviewed, what the disposition of those reviews were, and the average age of the alerts.

I'll add here, too, that it's important that your metrics are qualitative as well as quantitative. If you only ever ask about the average age of the alerts or the age of the oldest unclosed alert, you can end up encouraging the closure of alerts without adequate review which is not what you want and will ultimately get you into trouble.

I should also note here that these kinds of reports are a double-edged sword.

On one hand, I firmly believe that management needs to see them and that they need to exist. And I also believe as a former regulator that seeing that a company generates these kinds of reports goes a long way in giving the regulator confidence that the company is being well-managed from a compliance perspective.

However...If you have these types of reports and they are flagging a significant issue and that issue is not being addressed, then they actually work against you. Because now they show that you were aware of a significant compliance issue and that you failed to address it.

For example, if a report showed a tremendous spike in operational complaints and nothing was done to find the root cause of those complaints and fix it, then that shows a lack of appropriate supervision.

And if instead of addressing an issue with say a new product and its appropriateness for customers, the management response was to criticize compliance for reporting an increase in sales practice complaints, then in that case too having robust reporting would be to the detriment of the business.

In an ideal world, management and the board are well aware of the performance of the compliance department and they respect the role that compliance plays in their business, and support compliance and react appropriately when compliance identifies significant issues that need to be addressed.

Unfortunately, we do not always live in an ideal world.

But I will tell you that if you work for a company that doesn't want to hear about the performance of the compliance department and only wants to hear about revenue, growth, and profit, that you are very likely at some point in time going to be facing regulatory action or consumer lawsuits, depending on your industry. And if you are a compliance professional, I'd ask you whether this is really the kind of company you want to work for if they don't value what you bring to the table.

It is not easy to be the only one fighting the good fight. And trust me when I say that there are companies out there who do value their compliance staff appropriately.

So, summing it up: An ideal company will set the tone for compliance at the top. Management and the board will not just be focused on sales and profits but also on doing business "the right way." And that means that they will want to know about product performance, customer complaints, transaction monitoring, and all the rest that feed into a compliance program. Reporting will be done on a regular basis and done in such a way that performance can be effectively monitored and corrective action taken as needed. Focus will not only be on the numbers but also on the substance behind those numbers. The best management will understand that it's not just about having no complaints or closing alerts quickly if doing so hides underlying issues. And reports will be acted upon accordingly, not just generated and thrown in a drawer.

A NOTE ON STANDARDIZATION AND ASSIGNMENT OF RESPONSIBILITY

One more item to note before we dive into the various tools for building a regulatory compliance program and that's the importance of standardization. It's boring and it goes against everything your English teacher ever taught you, but using the same word to refer to the same person, concept, or requirement every single time is highly recommended.

For example, if I write a procedure and I say that the Training Compliance Officer is responsible for supervision of the Training Program, and then later I say that the Compliance Officer is responsible for the annual training certification, am I referring to the same person? Is the Training Compliance Officer the same as the Compliance Officer?

Maybe. Maybe not.

I've seen it go both ways.

And if I don't have a document somewhere naming who I mean when I refer to the Training Compliance Officer or the Compliance Officer then I've created a gap in the compliance program where no one will think that's their responsibility.

Also, is the training program referenced above the same as the annual training certification? Again, maybe, maybe not. I've seen that one go both ways as well.

The best compliance programs operate without a lot of ambiguity. They create roles and then use those roles throughout the policies and procedures and maintain in one very easy to find location the list of individuals who are assigned to each role. In my area of expertise there is an Anti-Money Laundering Compliance Officer (AMLCO) who is responsible for AML compliance. That person is named and they know they are the one who has to make sure that the policies and procedures are followed.

Also, the best compliance programs use standardized terminology as much as possible and those standardized terms are defined somewhere that is easy to find. A transaction is a transaction. It is not a transaction, a trade, a customer order, or whatever else might be somewhat equivalent. A customer is a customer not a customer, a client, an individual, a corporation, etc.

If different terms are used, there should be a reason for it.

I've seen policies and procedures where all defined terms were capitalized. I'm not sure that has to happen because you can end up with so many capitalized words that it becomes distracting, but do make sure that anyone modifying a policy or procedure or writing a new one knows about the standardized terms and uses them appropriately.

It's also a good idea when onboarding any new staff that they know how terms are used within your organization. Do not assume that because everyone in your company means X when they say "client" that the term has the same meaning at other companies. A standardized terms list can help get everyone on the same page so that there's no confusion.

Another point to make—and this is a bit outside the scope of our discussion here—but the more standardized your company data is across units and divisions, the better the compliance program you can build. I've dealt with financial institutions that have been around for a very long time and were built through a number of mergers and acquisitions over the years. Some of these companies have hundreds of customer transaction systems, each one with its own approach to customer data.

This makes, for example, identifying all client accounts with a nexus in Iran, a very time-consuming and imperfect process. It also severely impacts the ability to create a data warehouse. There are ways around this. You can map between different systems so that you figure out how one system records information and map it to another, but the mapping is rarely perfect. If one customer database lists income ranges of $25,001-$50,000 and the other lists $10,001 to $40,000 there's only so much you can do with that.

To the extent possible, I believe the compliance role should be the voice that argues for standardization. Regulatory expectations are evolving and it's hard to understand as a regulator why a company can't with the click of a few buttons generate a report of requested information.

(And I will add here for any of the regulators reading this that the data struggles that your regulated entities face, assuming they are not new entities built with attention to detail in the last few years, are immense. Most organizations cannot pivot on a dime when it comes to data. Some have to manually compile information across systems. Some have to wait for technology resources to be available to obtain information. If you're not dealing with a pre-existing standardized report, you're actually asking for a lot. This is something I probably did not appreciate enough when I was on the regulatory side of things.)

So, summing it up. Standardize, Standardize, Standardize. Assign responsibility to a specified role and make sure that one person, and only one person, is assigned to that role. (You can divvy this up by region or office or some other criteria so that the Branch Manager, for example, is a role in the policies and procedures but the Denver Branch Manager and the Chicago Branch Manager and the Boston Branch Manager each know that role applies to them for their location. What you don't want is there to be three people who could be the Branch Manager for a specific task.) Once you do this, keep the list of standardized terms and assigned roles somewhere easy to find and make sure that all new hires see it and absorb it. And when a new system is being built try to the extent possible to keep your data standardized as well.

YOUR COMPLIANCE TOOLS

The policies and procedures are the base upon which you build your compliance program. But then you need to choose how you will comply with each requirement. There are a number of tools available to you that I think are pretty standard across all industries. Those tools are:

- Codes of Conduct or Charters
- Employee Certifications
- Training
- Standardized Forms or Checklists
- Manual or Automated Monitoring Systems
- Controls
- Testing*

Let's walk through each one.

Codes of Conduct or Charters

A code of conduct is just what it sounds like. It sets forth the principles your company operates under. This is where you might state that you will treat all customers fairly, that you will not engage in illegal activity, that you will not discriminate against any individual based on their religion, race, gender, etc.

By their nature, codes of conduct are very high-level. They are best used to cover principles-based requirements. So, for example, FINRA Rule 2010 states that "A member, in the conduct of its business, shall observe high standards of commercial honor and just and equitable principles of trade."

Okay...What does that really mean, right? Over the years FINRA has issued guidance around this rule that sets forth specific issues like mark-ups that fall under the rule. (Some of which were later turned into their own rules.) But the general, principles-based requirement still exists on its own. And I in fact used it in a case when I had a firm lie to me in a way that didn't fall under any existing rule.

A firm that wanted to show compliance with this rule when there's really nothing to comply with other than the spirit of the requirement could incorporate it into their code of conduct. Any time there's any doubt about whether an activity is appropriate, this high-level standard applies.

In a similar way, sometimes you'll have a committee that has a compliance purpose. For example, it's always a good idea to have a new product committee that not only evaluates the business prospects of a new product but also the legal and compliance aspects. The charter that establishes such a committee can set forth the high-level compliance principles that are being addressed by the existence of that committee.

(I will say that I'm personally not a huge fan of using charters for this purpose, but I have seen it done. Usually I'd like to see that backed up somehow in the policies and procedures. For example, for a FINRA-member firm I'd expect to see a section of the policies and procedures for new product approval that mentions the existence of the committee.)

Employee Certifications

It's really not enough to write a policies and procedures manual and then shove it on a shelf somewhere. This is where a certification can come in handy. A certification is simply an affirmation by an employee that they have been provided and are familiar with a document, such as a policies and procedures manual, or that they are aware of their regulatory obligations as listed in the certification.

So, for example, when I was a registered broker I was given my firm's policies and procedures manual and asked to sign a certification that I had received the manual and was aware that I was required to comply with those policies and procedures. (Whether this was a realistic expectation or not is a completely different question. In my case, I don't think I ever made it past the first page of that four-inch binder. This was a couple years before I became a regulator myself and the firm I worked at was not very compliance-oriented.)

I've also seen certifications that employees signed that said they were aware that they were required to disclose outside business activities, that they could not have an outside brokerage account without prior approval from compliance, that they were required to notify compliance of any customer complaints they received as well as any bankruptcy they filed or any time they were arrested.

A certification is a good tool for making someone else acknowledge their responsibilities and putting the onus on them to make you aware of information you need to meet your regulatory obligations.

So in the case of a broker-dealer an individual's registration form may need to be amended if they are arrested, declare bankruptcy, or are the subject of a customer complaint. But how can the firm make that amendment if the individual in question doesn't tell them about it?

Same with outside business activities. Those are subject to disclosure and possibly supervision, but if the person conducting them never tells their firm then the firm has no good way to know there's activity they need to supervise.

Not taking proactive steps to ask employees if any of those circumstances apply can be seen as a failure to supervise. So a good compliance program figures out what employees need to disclose and then periodically, usually once a year, makes all employees certify that they are aware of the requirement to make that disclosure and that they have nothing to disclose or have already made all required disclosures.

Training

Some regulatory requirements rely very much on the action or knowledge of individual employees but they are too important to leave to a simple certification. In these instances training can be used.

Sometimes this is up to the business to determine and sometimes the training itself is a regulatory requirement. For example, FINRA Rule 3310, which applies to AML compliance, requires, in part, ongoing training related to anti-money laundering compliance be provided to appropriate personnel. Many other professions, such as the legal and medical professions, also require proof of continuing education.

When you have front-line employees whose actions drive your regulatory compliance then proactive training or continuing education becomes essential.

Standardized Forms or Checklists

A number of rule requirements, at least in the financial services industry, can be met through the use of standardized forms or checklists. This is why there is a customer new account form. And a standardized customer margin agreement. Built into those forms are a number of regulatory requirements related to customer information that must be collected and/or disclosures that must be made. Rather than rely on each individual to remember what information is required under a regulation, a standardized form takes the guesswork out of the process.

Checklists are another option. If there are ten items that must be completed by every new customer, better to have a checklist that lists those ten items than to ask every employee to remember what the ten items are.

The more you can standardized a process and take the guesswork out, the better.

Manual or Automated Monitoring Systems

Manual or automated monitoring systems are probably where the bulk of compliance monitoring happens. And they lie on top of everything we've already discussed. Because there's no point in having a certification or a training program or using a standardized form or checklist if you don't then monitor for compliance.

So you have the certification and then, depending on the size of the company, you establish a manual or automated monitoring system to ensure that the certification is completed by every employee.

In addition to using a monitoring system to confirm completion of certifications, training, forms, and checklists, many regulatory requirements will only be met through the use of a manual or automated monitoring system. For financial services, this would include requirements around charges to customers, trading, suspicious activity, and more.

A manual system is just what it sounds like. It's done by an individual, by hand. They might use something like an Excel spreadsheet, but the person is responsible for performing the monitoring tasks. For a small firm with twenty employees there's no point in paying for an automated system that monitors for code of conduct certification every year. (I mean, you could. But chances are the expense will make it cost-prohibitive.) So in that case someone is assigned to take a list of the twenty employees and collect their signed certifications by March 31st of every year.

An automated system still will rely heavily on individuals but the monitoring will be done via computer. Let's take the annual code of conduct as an example. In an automated monitoring system, employees would be asked to complete their code of conduct certification online. There would likely be an automated email that is sent to all employees that is triggered by an individual telling the system to send it. The employees would then use a link from the email to go complete their certification. Those who hadn't completed it within X number of days would likely receive a follow-up notice that was system-generated. After Y number of days the individual responsible for the process would then generate a report of those who still had not completed the certification and follow-up with them in-person or with their supervisors, depending on the size of the organization.

I can't think of a single automated monitoring system that doesn't require some level of individual interaction either to trigger the system to begin or to follow-up on exceptions. Perhaps someday a system like that could be 100% automated, but humans are pretty crafty and they find ways around things they don't want to do. So I personally would never rely on a system being completely automated.

Controls

Controls can on the other hand be completely automated. In this context I think of a control as something you can prohibit from happening through a computerized system. So this is the situation where you're not allowed to purchase a product without providing a mailing address. Or you're not allowed to open a new account without completing a new account form.

Controls are best used for situations where something *must* occur and there is no ambiguity about it.

So, for example, if you're a business in the U.S. there are certain countries that you cannot do business with without violating U.S. law. For those countries you could program a customer sales system to prevent any customer from providing an address in that country. Or you could ask for a customer's residency country and prohibit the opening of any account where that country is listed as the country of residence. (Sanctions regulations are in reality a little more tricky to comply with than that, but you get the idea.)

Or, as another example, which happens to be a tax example more than a compliance example, I wasn't allowed to open a vendor account with Apple until I had agreed to their terms of service, provided tax information that they verified, and listed a valid bank account. There was no way for me to list my products with them until those steps had been completed. Those requirements were all automated.

The one thing to be careful of with controls is that the information you require is actually required. I have more than once seen a system circumvented when a control was put in place that the users at least did not feel should be required. For example, I myself will do this on sites that want my phone number when I don't think they need it. They have a control in place that I can't place an order with them unless I provide a phone number, so I end up providing one like (123) 456-7890 to get around it, which makes it useless.

If you are using controls, periodically monitor to make sure that they're set up in such a way that they can't be subverted.

One way to do this is to review the data you're receiving. I remember doing an exam once and asking for an output of information into an Excel spreadsheet and finding within 30 seconds that the firm's registered representatives had found a workaround for a required field because when I grouped the answers provided for that field the top result was a garbage answer. Something like 1111.

Because the same garbage answer had been provided five hundred times it was clear this was a workaround that had been passed from representative to representative.

You do not want something like that happening with a required control. So even though you can automate the control, you still need to have an individual check that it's working.

Testing

That leads to our last tool, which is testing of the compliance system. Testing involves trying the program to see if it's working properly. So trying to open an account for a prohibited customer type or customer in a prohibited geography. Or having someone ask a front-line employee to somehow do something that should be prohibited under policy or procedure.

This one is rarely used as a primary compliance tool in my world because you can usually use one of the tools above to better effect. But when there is a requirement to periodically review the sufficiency of the compliance program then testing becomes one of the ways to meet that requirement. You're basically looking to see if what you've put in place does what it's supposed to do.

THE ROLE OF THE AUDIT, RISK, AND LEGAL DEPARTMENTS

I just mentioned testing. Sometimes testing isn't done by compliance itself but by audit or even risk. So I wanted to discuss briefly how audit, risk, and legal interact with compliance in a larger organization, keeping in mind that there are no firm lines around this and it may vary from organization to organization.

If you look at this from a high-level perspective there's the regulator who establishes the regulatory requirements and (hopefully) periodically conducts exams to make sure that those requirements are being followed.

Legal will monitor for changes or interpretations to those regulatory requirements and may also serve as an intermediary with the regulator when specific interpretations of requirements are needed. They may also advise compliance on whether the established compliance program meets the regulatory requirements. Depending on the entity legal staff may be part of the compliance department or they may be a separate department.

Risk may also be a part of the compliance department or separate. When separate risk is generally Enterprise Risk Management and compliance risk is just one type of risk that they oversee. Risk will provide input to compliance about the entity's risk tolerance, which may impact monitoring systems, for example, and may conduct its own supplementary testing.

Audit also has a broader remit than just regulatory compliance. A lot of their focus is on financial controls, but they may also test and monitor other corporate functions, including some of those that fall under the purview of the compliance department. Depending on the regulator and the regulatory environment, audit may perform more frequent testing than the regulator does.

It's generally a good idea to have either an internal or external mock exam in anticipation of a regulatory exam, although not required.

On a day-to-day basis the compliance function is responsible for monitoring for compliance with all of the entity's regulatory requirements and testing the compliance systems.

The business, which is subject to the policies and procedures established by the compliance department, is also responsible for daily compliance. The employees that work in the business are the ones who actually perform the specific requirements, such as completion of new account forms, that are mandated by those policies and procedures.

All of these pieces have to work together for there to be an effective compliance program. And no component can make up for the responsibility of any other component. So front-line employees must perform their tasks. Their managers must ensure that those tasks are done. Compliance must monitor those activities and catch what slips through the cracks. Risk and legal must work with compliance to establish an effective program. And then audit and the regulator must periodically perform exams to make sure that it's functioning as expected.

Nothing will ever be 100%. The regulator and auditor will rarely test every single transaction or event. It's simply not possible and not feasible. And a compliance program should not expect 100% perfection either. The goal is a reasonable level of compliance where what is reasonable is very much driven by potential harm and industry expectation.

ADDITIONAL CONSIDERATIONS

We just walked through the primary tools that you can use to build a regulatory compliance program, but buried within those tools are some additional concepts that I wanted to call out in more detail. Specifically, sampling, risk-based monitoring, exception reports, outsourcing, separation of duties, and timeliness of reviews. In and of themselves they are not tools for building a compliance program, but they are important factors in doing so nonetheless.

Let's jump right in with sampling.

SAMPLING

When you're small it's easy to do a hundred percent sampling. If you open five accounts a month then it takes almost no time to look at each new account form to make sure that it was fully completed and that the answers to every question made sense. But at some point a one hundred percent manual review becomes unfeasible.

That's when you either need to move to an automated system or you need to start sampling.

So, for example, you could implement an online new account form that must be completed and where answers must be provided to each and every question and there are controls around acceptable answers.

Or you could continue with your manual review but start reviewing only a subset of new account forms instead of all of them.

Now, as I type this I cringe, because I'm pretty

sure that I would not have been okay as an examiner with a firm that sampled its new account forms. I would have expected 100% review of those by a branch manager or the use of an automated system. So that's where regulatory expectations come into play. You have to know where sampling will be accepted and where it won't.

And because I can't seem to take off my hard-ass regulator hat at the moment, let me switch the example to an industry I didn't work in: food safety.

In an ideal world you would sample every single can of product that is going to be distributed to someone for consumption right before you seal up the can. But I imagine that's a very costly process and that the time and effort required to do that level of sampling isn't feasible. Best to sample earlier in the process when ingredients are in their raw form and then when everything has been combined together and is still in one big vat.

But, if it were me, I'd probably also want to take a sample of the absolute finished product as well. So maybe I'd pull 1 can in 1,000 off the finished product assembly line and sample it for any contaminants and to make sure the ingredients are what we said they were.

Because I'm not using any special criteria to make my choice of which can to examine, that's basic sampling. It's just, grab one off the shelf, and see what you see.

One of the key questions with sampling is: what sample size should you pull?

The answer to that question is going to be driven by your industry.

There are two factors to consider. The first is the accepted error rate for the industry. How many errors are you willing to let slip by without being identified?

I did an internet search on the acceptable error rate in the pharmaceutical industry for example and found an article about filling prescriptions that stated that the target accuracy level was 99.7% for that industry, meaning they were willing to accept an error rate of .3%.

In financial services regulation, we generally used 10% as the level at which an issue was considered material and warranted formal action.

The other part of that determination is how certain you want to be that your error rate is less than the targeted level.

So do you want to be 98% certain that your error rate is 10% or less? Or do you want to be 95% certain that your error rate is 10% or less?

If you decide you want to be 99.99% certain that your error rate is 1% or less you are going to be taking a much, much larger sample than someone who decides they want to be 95% certain that the error rate is 10% or less.

Using these two numbers (certainty and error rate) you can then get a sample size based upon your total population.

You'll find that as the total population increases that sample size reaches a plateau. (I believe the technical term is an asymptote.) So for any given confidence level and error rate there is a maximum sample size that you need to take.

Essentially what you're saying is "If I take this

many samples and find nothing then I can be X% certain that the error rate in my population is no greater than Y%." If Y% is an acceptable number for you and X% is a high enough confidence level it doesn't mean that you're error free but it does mean that you're within acceptable bounds.

That's as far into the math as I'm going to get here. If you want to dig into this more there are plenty of sources out there on how to calculate a sample size based on the confidence level you want and the error rate you're willing to accept.

The key to effective sampling though is to take *random* samples of your population.

Ideally you have a list of everything you want to sample, let's say 1,000 cans of product or 1,000 new account forms. You then randomly select a starting point. (A random number generator is the best way to do this.) And then you divide your total population, of 1,000 in this case, by your sample size, let's say 60. That gets you the number 17. Go to your randomly-selected starting point and then choose every 17th item from your list until you have sixty items in your sample. This may require you to circle back to the beginning or go past your starting point once.

By making your sample random, even though you didn't test all 1,000 items in your sample you can state with X% certainty what the potential error rate in that population is.

But the key is that the sample must be random. You cannot throw out any item in the sample. So I can't say, "Oh, let's not review that new account form because it's for an LLC and not an individual."

The minute you do that, you mess up the randomness of your sample and all the statistics go out the window.

Which leads us to our next topic: risk-based monitoring.

RISK-BASED MONITORING

Risk-based monitoring focuses in on those areas where there is believed to be additional risk.

Let me give an example from my FINRA days.

Not all firms are created equal. Some are higher risk than others either because of the business they do or the individuals they employ.

When I was at FINRA all firms were reviewed on a four-year cycle. So no matter what the firm or what its risk level it was going to get a regulatory exam every four years. (Unless it was located internationally and then I think the default was six years.) So overall we had 100% sampling to make sure that we weren't missing something.

But for a higher-risk firm you do not want to let activity go for four years without a review. It is not reasonable to let the largest firms in the industry go that long without an exam. Nor is it reasonable to ignore the fact that some firms tend to attract more problematic registered representatives. Or the fact that not all securities products are created equal. Some are much more prone to abuse than others.

So what FINRA did when I was there was start with a pure hundred-percent sampling approach. All firms were examined every four years regardless of revenue, size, etc. And then FINRA added to that a risk-based monitoring approach where some firms were reviewed more frequently based on their size, business, and other risk factors.

This was the best of both worlds in my opinion. We didn't let anything slide, but we focused most of our efforts on the firms most likely to yield a result.

I am a firm believer in risk-based monitoring as a way to target your efforts where they're most likely needed. However, you don't know what you don't know so I would also encourage you to periodically make sure that you've randomly sampled the entire population.

For example, at FINRA we could have an examiner walk into an office expecting a half-day exam because the office showed almost no revenue only to find that the registered representative was running a Ponzi scheme related to real estate investment out of the same location. Something the examiner would never know without going on-site.

So focus your efforts where they make the most sense, but don't ignore any aspect of your business forever.

In financial services this is where, for example, you have Enhanced Due Diligence AML requirements for certain high-risk accounts where you perform more documentation and review than you would on a normal account.

Let me think of a few non-finance examples for this as well.

With car manufacturing I would think that brakes, steering, engine, air bags, and tires are areas of higher risk than say carpeting, audio systems, and drink holders. Sure, you want them all to work, but if I had limited resources to monitor for safety compliance I would be focused on the parts of the car that if they don't work right could kill someone. But at the same time I'd still occasionally want to make sure that someone hadn't tried to cut a corner and ordered third-rate carcinogenic carpeting.

With food manufacturing, I would probably consider bagged fresh produce higher risk than frozen produce. There are occasional food-borne illness outbreaks for frozen products but my gut feel is that the number of food-borne illness outbreaks for bagged lettuce, for example, are far higher.

Even within a high-risk business in a high-risk industry you will still likely have higher risk areas that deserve additional resources or compliance focus.

EXCEPTION REPORTS

Exception reports are actually part of an automated monitoring system, but I want to call them out separately because they have a special role in compliance.

An exception report can be a 100% review for a certain issue that then lists out all activity that failed to meet the requirement. So, in our example about completion of the code of conduct certification, there might be an automated system that monitors for completion and then a monthly exception report that lists all individuals who didn't complete the certification.

Exception reports work best with yes or no type rules like this. Everyone is required to complete the certification. Anyone on that exception report is someone who has not done what they were required to do.

In the broker-dealer space clearing firms often provide a large number of exception reports that their firms can use. One that I always reviewed as an examiner was the 5% report that showed all customer transactions where the customer paid more than 5% in a commission or mark-up/mark-down for the transaction. (Another good example of an industry standard that was basically a rule by the time I was an examiner.)

While a charge of over 5% was sometimes justified, the exception report was a quick way to check each and every transaction to see if it exceeded the limit of what was considered acceptable for the average transaction so that compliance (or the regulator) could then focus in on only those transactions that were potentially violations.

(I should note here that in some instances a charge of less than 5% would have still been problematic but that was a rare circumstance to identify at your average firm.)

Exception reports are great, but they need to be reviewed. They are not where things stop, they are a tool for compliance to use in its monitoring. From there, a person needs to determine how to handle the activity flagged by the report.

In our code of conduct example, maybe the person was fired January 1st before they could sign the certification for the year. So even though the report shows them as not having signed, that's acceptable.

Also, it's important when an issue is flagged by an exception report (or otherwise) that someone take the steps to identify the root cause. Let's talk about that next.

ROOT CAUSE ANALYSIS

A good compliance program is not just reactive but also proactive. So it is not enough to say, "These ten people didn't sign their certification." A good compliance program will also demand of its staff that they ask why violations are occurring.

Let me give a weird example.

Years ago I went into a firm and I noticed that a large number of new accounts were being charged tax withholding on their sales transactions. That can happen if someone opens an account but hasn't provided the correct tax forms. So maybe it was nothing. But it was odd enough I decided to dig in further.

What I found was that this only happened in one particular branch office of that firm. And that it only was happening with a handful of brokers in that office.

Now, according to the law the clearing firm had done what they needed to do. When there wasn't a tax form on file for an account and the account sold and made a profit on a stock they withheld 30%.

But...

Long story short, it turns out that exception that was occurring in those accounts was a sign of unauthorized trading. That handful of representatives had obtained information on these customers through a prior broker-dealer and had then used that information to open new accounts for these people and put through trades in their name. If the trade lost money, they cancelled it. If the trade made money, they called up the customer and convinced them to pay for it since, hey, they'd made money, hadn't they?

If I hadn't dug into that pattern of activity, those unauthorized trades would've continued to be made.

That's an extreme example. But let's take the code of certification example from above. Let's say there are ten that aren't completed. But when you dig in you realize that all ten are for one specific department. That is a red flag in my opinion that there is an issue in that department. Whether it is over-work so things are slipping through the cracks or whether it is an active discouragement of corporate compliance, it's an indicator of a bigger issue.

So anytime you have a compliance problem or see exceptions happening, at least try to take a minute and dig in and see if there's more to it. Sometimes people forget to do a training and that's all it is. Sometimes they miss that something is not allowed. But often there is a small pocket within the larger organization that needs to be dealt with. It's not always sinister. But if it's not dealt with, the issues will continue.

OUTSOURCING

Sometimes it makes the most sense to find someone else to handle a certain aspect of your regulatory compliance program. For example, a number of firms use an outside source to create and deliver their AML training to their employees. It creates a nice standardized product and lets someone else manage the bulk of the notification and tracking that's required in an AML training program.

Others outsource their quarterly financial filings. Or their advertising review.

There is nothing wrong with outsourcing a responsibility like that. And sometimes it leads to better compliance.

However, outsourcing does not mean that you can simply wash your hands and walk away from your responsibility. So if you are going to outsource your responsibility for compliance in a particular area you basically end up trading off one compliance obligation (in the first example above, the training of employees on AML) for another compliance obligation (making sure that the outside entity you paid to make sure that training happened did what you paid them to do).

And you still need to be involved if things aren't working. So if that outside entity sends notice to all of your employees that they need to take the training and they don't take it, that's on your business not on theirs. You at the end of the day have that obligation, not them.

Also keep in mind that certain activities do not outsource well. There are a number of regulatory requirements around the world related to the protection of personal information and it is possible that if you haven't structured your disclosures properly that you are not in fact allowed to outsource certain activities.

Other activities are considered too sensitive to outsource. Either they are too central to your business to risk it on an outside entity or they are not allowed to be outsourced. No outsourcing decision should be made lightly.

Before your company outsources any responsibility, be sure to have your legal, risk, and compliance departments confirm that you can and should do so. And then make sure that your compliance program includes supervision of the outsourced activity to make sure that it's being done to the required standard.

SEPARATION OF DUTIES

When assigning an individual to supervise an activity for regulatory compliance purposes, to the extent possible do not assign someone to supervise themselves.

In the financial services world we have what are called producing branch managers. These are individuals who are responsible for supervising a branch office. Part of their duties might, for example, include reviewing all transactions for their branch for suitability and reviewing all correspondence with customers of the branch. But a producing branch manager is also someone who has their own clients.

And if you create a compliance program that has the branch manager as responsible for signing off on all branch activity without establishing a separate review for the activity of the producing branch manager you have just created a system with a gigantic flaw in it. Because if that producing branch manager is in any way unethical, there is no one there to review and flag their activity.

In the same way that you don't have someone who writes your checks reconcile your corporate bank account, don't put someone in charge of themselves.

Also, be careful that you don't put someone who reports to an individual in charge of monitoring that individual's activity. It's the rare individual who will tell on the person who can fire them.

The separation of duties can be a challenge in a smaller business or niche departments, but to the extent that you can manage it, do so. We all want to believe in the honesty and integrity of the people we work with, but it is that very trust that dishonest people abuse. So trust, but verify.

TIMELINESS VS.
THOROUGHNESS OF REVIEWS

Sometimes you will have timeframes set forth in a regulation that you must meet. For example, broker-dealers have specified timeframes for filing customer complaint information that must be met. But often compliance reviews are not governed by specific timeframes. This is especially true for activity monitoring.

I cannot count the number of firms I have seen put in place an AML or OFAC monitoring system who then fell hopelessly behind in processing the alerts that that system generated. It is very common for a new alert system to overwhelm existing resources while the system is being fine-tuned.

To me, that represents a flaw in the system and is not the correct way to approach this kind of monitoring.

As we discussed above, there are higher risk areas within any business. And within that higher risk there are gradations of risk. So for AML purposes a cash-intensive business situated in a high-risk foreign jurisdiction and owned by a series of corporations where the ultimate ownership is masked is far higher risk than that same cash-intensive business situated in Idaho where the same family has owned the company for a hundred years. Both are cash-intensive, but one has far more red flags than the other.

Now sometimes you don't have a choice but to review all transactions that are flagged by the system. Cash transactions are probably one of those. If you process a cash transaction over a set amount you must file that transaction so you need to generate that alert. There's no wiggle room.

But often with suitability monitoring or suspicious activity monitoring those lines are not as clear. And in my opinion, and this is only my opinion, I think it is better to set a higher threshold for what is flagged initially and review those alerts within thirty days of the alert being generated than to set a lower threshold and not review an alert for eight, nine, ten months or more.

Sure, you maybe miss something using a higher threshold. But you make up for that in catching the activity in time for it to actually matter.

And ideally over time with a new monitoring system you begin to understand what is creating false alerts and you can then adjust that system to remove those false alerts. When you do so you can then lower your thresholds so that you're still reviewing the same number of alerts as at the start but the quality of those alerts is higher.

Putting on my regulator hat, the one place where I personally would not accept that sort of decision was if it were clear that the higher threshold had been established simply because the company wasn't willing to spend enough money to meet its compliance obligations.

This once more comes back to industry practice and what everyone else has in place. If you have one compliance person at your firm and other firms of a similar size and risk-level have a department of ten in place, and you're not able to keep up with your compliance responsibilities, that will be a hit against you for failing to establish an adequate compliance program.

So have sufficient resources in place and then find that balance between timeliness of review and extent of the reviews you can complete. Target the highest-risk areas first. Refine your monitoring over time. And then broaden. Don't just dive in from day one. You'll spend years and lots and lots of money recovering from that mistake.

CONCLUSION

Alright. So that's basically it.

You need to understand what your regulatory requirements are, written and unwritten. You need to then create a compliance program that uses as its base a set of written policies and procedures that are easy to follow and accessible. And then you need to use the compliance tool that makes the most sense for each requirement, while leveraging available options like sampling, risk-based monitoring, and outsourcing.

This cannot be a static program that you establish once and then forget. It is constantly changing and evolving as regulatory requirements, industry standards, and your business activities change.

And keep in mind that for a truly successful compliance program you need senior management that believes in the value of the program, provides it with adequate resources, and places regulatory compliance on a level of importance equal to profitability. And even then you will never achieve 100% compliance all the time. Not without grinding your business to a halt.

The goal is to reasonably attempt to comply with your requirements and to prioritize those that are zero-sum, meaning you will pay a fine if you violate them no matter what, those that are a priority for your regulator, and those that are the most important with respect to reputational risk and customer harm.

It's all a balancing act. And the best compliance personnel are masters at it.

Good luck.

INDEX

ABOUT THE AUTHOR

M.L. (Muffie) Humphrey is a former stockbroker with degrees in Economics, Anthropology, and Psychology from Stanford and an MBA from Wharton who spent close to twenty years as a regulator and consultant in the financial services industry.

You can reach her at
mlhumphreywriter@gmail.com or
at mlhumphrey.com.